URBAN GARDENING
AND FARMING
FOR TEENS™

BEEKEEPING

HARVEST YOUR OWN HONEY

ALEXANDRA HANSON-HARDING

ROSEN
PUBLISHING®

New York

Published in 2014 by The Rosen Publishing Group, Inc.
29 East 21st Street, New York, NY 10010

Library of Congress Cataloging-in-Publication Data

Hanson-Harding, Alexandra.
Beekeeping: harvest your own honey/Alexandra Hanson-Harding.
    p. cm.—(Urban gardening and farming for teens)
ISBN 978-1-4777-1778-3 ((library binding))
1. Bee culture. I. Title. II. Series: Urban gardening and farming for teens.
SF523.H244 2014
638'.1—dc23
                                                                    2013017443

Manufactured in the United States of America

CPSIA Compliance Information: Batch #W14YA: For further information, contact Rosen Publishing, New York, New York, at 1-800-237-9932.

Contents

4 INTRODUCTION

7 CHAPTER ONE
WHAT'S THE BUZZ ABOUT BEES?

13 CHAPTER TWO
MEET THE HONEYBEE

20 CHAPTER THREE
BECOMING A BEEKEEPER

30 CHAPTER FOUR
TROUBLESHOOTING BEEKEEPING

36 CHAPTER FIVE
ALL ABOUT HONEY

43 CHAPTER SIX
WHAT'S THE FUTURE FOR BEES?

49 GLOSSARY

51 FOR MORE INFORMATION

54 FOR FURTHER READING

56 BIBLIOGRAPHY

61 INDEX

Introduction

enry Miller is only a teenager. But the Deming, Washington, boy owns his own business, Henry's Humdingers. The company sells a line of special honey called Stingers. The raw, spicy honey comes in such flavors as Naughty Nana, Grumpy Grandpa, and Phoebe's Fireball. It is used for making barbecue sauces and generally spicing things up! His honeys are available in more than thirty states and on the Internet.

How did he start? At eleven, Henry met a beekeeper who inspired him to start his own hives. He lives in a rural area, so he had room for hives, and he has a helpful family. He donates part of his sales to the Foundation for the Preservation of Honey Bees. He told *Grow Northwest* magazine, "There are so many mysteries about bees."

Like Henry, people have long been drawn to the mystery of the honeybee, or *Apis mellifera*. Honeybees, their sweet syrup, and their complex hives have long been a source of fascination. They played a role in the religious myths of many ancient cultures. They have often been used as a symbol for the ultimate cooperative society.

Honeybees are native to Africa, the Middle East, and Europe. Eight-thousand-year-old cave paintings of honey hunters have been discovered in Valencia, Spain. Ancient Egyptians kept honeybees. Greek and Roman writers such as Herodotus and Pliny

Young beekeeper and entrepreneur Henry Miller shows off some of his bees while dressed in a beekeeping outfit.

observed them carefully (although they did get a few facts, such as assuming that the workers were male, and not female, wrong). Since that time, writers have been writing poetically about the details of bee life.

In the 1600s, Europeans brought honeybees to North America, where they made themselves right at home. Approximately four thousand bee species are native to North America, but honeybees proved so flexible and their honey such a treasure that their value quickly became clear.

According to the National Honey Board, one-third of the total human diet is derived from insect-pollinated plants. The U.S. Department of Agriculture (USDA) estimates that honeybees alone are responsible for 80 percent of insect crop pollination. According to the Foundation for the Preservation of Honey Bees, "Honeybees are premier pollinators because they are available throughout the growing season, they pollinate a wide range of crops, and they can be concentrated whenever and wherever they are needed."

Unfortunately, the honeybee population has been shrinking in recent years. Luckily, people like Henry Miller are coming to their aid. Many are setting up their own apiaries (bee homes) in backyard gardens, on city rooftops, and even in schools. The elegant Waldorf-Astoria Hotel in New York City has six hives on its roof.

Others are writing letters, planting bee-friendly gardens, and spreading the word about the importance of bees. Helping bees is a great way to connect to the environment as a family, school, or group project. By learning more about honeybees, people reap the sweet reward of discovering a fascinating world that we rely on every time we eat a tasty handful of almonds, bite into a juicy apple, or spread golden honey on toast. As bee scientist Karl von Frisch wrote in his book *Bees: Their Vision, Chemical Senses, and Language*, "The bee's life is like a magic well: the more you draw from it, the more it fills with water."

CHAPTER ONE

WHAT'S THE BUZZ ABOUT BEES?

Honeybees make honey, of course. But they are even more valuable for their ability to pollinate crops. What is pollination? Many plant foods we eat, including seeds, nuts, berries, and fruits, are created from a union of male and female germ cells. But plants are stuck in the ground. So how do these germ cells unite? One answer is pollen, a powder containing male germ cells that comes from the male part of the flower, called the stamen. When pollen lands on a pistil (a female part), it fertilizes it. That allows new plants to grow.

The honeybee brings pollen from male to female plant parts when it flies from one flower to the next in the process of gathering nectar, a sweet liquid the flowers make to tempt these little helpers. The pollen sticks to the hairy bodies of the bees and then rubs off on other flowers. Honeybees pollinate more than ninety crops in the United States alone, according to the Associated Press.

A worker bee gathers sweet nectar and dusty pollen from a yellow flower. As the bee moves to other flowers, it will pollinate them so that they can create new plants.

BEES ARE VALUABLE

According to science news Web site Phys.org, German researchers measured the value of sixty different crops that require pollination. They learned that the value of pollination rose from about $200 billion in 1993 to $350 billion in 2009. They found that the production costs of plants that need pollination—including coffee and cocoa—have gone up much faster than those that don't, such as rice or grains. Why? The researchers believe that when too much habitat is taken away from insects and too much insecticide is sprayed on fields, honeybees disappear. Then it costs extra money to hire bees to do the pollinating. "This [study] could encourage incentives for the protection of insects

8

and their pollination services," said Sven Lautenbach, one of the researchers.

BEES ON THE ROAD

Many large farms in heavily agricultural locations rely on professional beekeepers, who bring their bees in on trucks. The bees spend a few weeks in an area and pollinate the plants. Then the trucks roll on to other locations.

One crop that needs bees is California almonds. About 80 percent of the world's almonds are grown in central California. The crop is worth about $3 billion a year, according to the National Agricultural Statistics Service (NASS). Every spring, more than 2.6 million colonies of honeybees are needed to pollinate the almonds, according to the Department of Entomology and Nematology at the University of California, Davis. Most of these bees are brought to California each spring on trucks from as far away as Florida.

Some environmentalists are not big fans of the practice.

Beekeeper and bee scientist Dr. Gordon Wardell checks the health of a hive in an almond orchard in Lost Hills, California. Without bees, the state's valuable almond crop could be destroyed.

That's because the bees are often fed corn syrup instead of their own honey. Sometimes the queen's wings are clipped so that she can't escape. The hives are also kept close together, so disease can spread quickly. Traveling thousands of miles (kilometers) on

FOR A SWEET NEW YEAR

Beekeeping used to be, and still is, illegal in some places. Only in 2010 was beekeeping made legal in New York City, for instance. Bees have adapted successfully to city life and help keep local parks and gardens flourishing. Now there is a beekeeping boom. Much of the honey produced is sold in the fall. That's because the demand for honey peaks around the Jewish new year holiday of Rosh Hashanah. Traditionally honey is eaten with apple slices or is baked

in rich honey cake. It is a symbol of happiness. As Brooklyn beekeeper Rachel Greene told the *New York Daily News*, "Rosh Hashanah is the time to think about your future, your past, and what you can do differently. Bees are part of the future. The world needs them."

Apples and sweet honey are a traditional Rosh Hashanah treat, shown here with pomegranates and bread. Locally grown honey makes the holiday even more special for some families.

the highway to new locations can stress the bees, too. Commercial beekeepers sometimes coat the bees with chemicals that control bee diseases. These chemicals may be unhealthy in the long run and may seep into the bees' honey. Fans of wild, pure honey are concerned that this could undermine the health benefits and distinctive taste that good honey has.

THE POWER OF HOMESTEAD BEEKEEPING

However, many beekeepers are committed to taking a more natural approach to their hives. Often they are called "hobby" or "homestead" beekeepers because they may have only a few hives instead of hundreds—or thousands. Most homestead

New backyard beekeeper Grace Fenstermacher picks up her first package of bees in Denver, Colorado, in May 2013. Each package holds ten thousand workers and drones and one queen.

beekeepers do not truck their hives. Even First Lady Michelle Obama has a hive of bees at the White House!

One example of a homestead beekeeper is nineteen-year-old Caroline Lowery. In 2012, she was named the South Carolina Junior Beekeeper of the Year. After an internship at the USDA's Honeybee Research Laboratory in Maryland, she started two hives of her own. "My internship really gave me the confidence to handle beekeeping on my own. It allowed me the opportunity to get into a hive and be covered in bees and not be scared," Lowery told the Charleston, South Carolina, *Post and Courier*. She wrote about her bees on her blog *Becoming Queen Bee*.

Lowery had a tough experience that many beginning bee-keepers have: one of her two hives died. But, now at college, she thinks the experience helped her. She joined a student gardening association that received money to start beehives in the garden. She told the *Post and Courier*, "When one beehive dies, you get three more hives the next spring. Take failure, move on, and learn from it. Don't dwell. Time is a powerful thing."

Some schools are keeping bees, too. There are active hives at a number of Waldorf schools, where students learn a kind of natural gardening called biodynamic farming. Highland Hall Waldorf School in Northridge, California, for instance, has five beehives actively pollinating a large garden. The hives are carefully placed away from the pathways that students normally use. The students learn how to care for and about bees.

CHAPTER TWO

MEET THE HONEYBEE

More than twenty thousand different kinds of bees live around the world. Some have stingers. Others do not. Some are solitary. This type of bee will create its own nest and put in food for each larva. Other bees are semi-social. They live in clusters and at times cooperate.

But of all the bees, the honeybees are the most social. They live in huge colonies of up to about sixty thousand bees. They are so cooperative that they have been called a superorganism—a mass group of organisms that depend on one another and devote their lives to the common good. Unlike many other bee-hives, the hives of honeybees can survive winters and start again in the spring.

WHAT IS A HONEYBEE?

A honeybee is a member of the same insect family as wasps. Like all insects, it has six legs and three main body parts: head,

A bee's main body parts—including the head, thorax, and abdomen—can be clearly seen here. The wings and legs emerge from the thorax, the central section of the body.

thorax, and abdomen. Its exoskeleton (outside skeleton) is made of small pieces of a hard material called chitin. A bee's body is entirely covered in tiny, forked hairs. This fuzz traps pollen and helps the bee stay warm in winter.

Honeybees' heads include antennae, which they use for touching and smelling; mouthparts; and eyes. They have two compound eyes, each made up of about 150 eye parts called ommatidia. The bees see patterns and colors, including ultraviolet light, which humans can't see. They also have three tiny eyes on top of their heads called ocelli. These detect light levels, letting them find their way in the dark hives. Their mouthparts include jawlike mandibles, which they use for chewing wax into usable shapes, such as hexagonal cells and caps for the cells. Their long tongues can loop deep down into the center of flowers to gather nectar.

Attached to the thorax, or middle part of the honeybee, are two sets of strong wings and six legs. The wings can hook together for added strength when flying. Their wings flap eleven thousand times per minute. Their back legs are built to carry as much pollen as possible; they even have pollen buckets to trap extra grains of the protein-rich powder.

The abdomen of bees contains most of their organs. It also contains their stingers. Honeybees can only sting large creatures like mammals once. Their stingers are barbed and tear off when they sting, killing the bees.

WHAT IS A HIVE?

A hive is where a honeybee lives, stores food, and grows a new generation. In nature, hives can exist in the hollows of trees and other secluded spots. Bees also live quite happily in hives made up of man-made frames. These are designed to give the bees just the right amount of space so that they are tightly—but not too tightly—packed together.

Worker bees have special wax glands in their stomachs. They chew the wax into rows and rows of waxy sheets divided into small hexagons. They raise the young and store honey in these cells.

Because infection can spread quickly in a hive, dirt is cleared away at a fast pace. If a bee returns from a foraging trip feeling dirty, other bees will quickly dust it off. Queens will not lay eggs

Worker bees busily prepare the empty hexagonal cells in a hive. The queen is in the center.

in a dirty cell. Even in winter, bees will wait for days until it is warm enough for them to fly outside to go to the bathroom. Most bees die outside of the nest, but if one accidentally dies inside, others will slowly and carefully push its body out of the hive.

MEET THE BEE FAMILY

Three types of bees live in a honeybee colony: queens, drones, and workers. But first, they all start as eggs. A bee's life starts when the queen bee lays a tiny, white, rice-shaped egg in a cell. She will lay a male egg in a larger cell and a female egg in a smaller one. The word "brood" refers to the developing, immature bees within the colony.

After about three days, the eggs hatch into semicircular larvae. Young worker bees will feed them a special milky substance called royal jelly, which they secrete from glands in their heads, and then a honey and pollen blend called beebread. If they are raising a new queen, they feed her only royal jelly. The larvae grow rapidly. After a few days, they stop eating. Worker bees seal them over with wax. Once sealed, the larvae spin cocoons around themselves and become pupae.

Under their wax caps, the pupae change. They develop into adult bees. This process is called complete metamorphosis. When mature, the bees push their way out of the wax caps and begin their adult lives.

QUEEN BEE AND DRONES

A queen is a hive's most precious resident. She is made, not born. If a new queen is needed, workers feed several ordinary eggs nothing but royal jelly. A queen can live for two years or more. She grows much larger than the other bees. She lays as many as two thousand eggs a day! Her pheromones

A queen bee is noticeable because she is considerably larger than the workers that surround her. Here, the bees gather on wax-capped cells.

(chemical messengers) set the tone for the hive, letting the bees know that all is well.

Not long after she becomes an adult, the queen flies out of the nest followed by drones (males). In the air, a number of drones will mate with her. She will store their sperm in a part of her body called a spermatheca. She will use the sperm to create female worker bees for the rest of her life. The queen also lays unfertilized eggs, which develop into male drones.

Unlike female worker bees, drones don't work. But if they are one of the drones "lucky" enough to impregnate the queen, their genitals get ripped off their bodies by the process of mating and they die. In the fall, when the weather gets colder, workers will kick the surviving drones out of the hive to die because of their uselessness. So their easy life is a precarious one.

THE WAGGLE DANCE

When foraging bees find a good source of bee-friendly flowers, they often do a special dance when they return to the hive. This helps other bees find the nectar, too. If the dance is round, it means nectar is nearby. If it's a waggling dance, it means that nectar is farther away. The bee makes figure eights and other patterns to give directions. The longer the bee dances, the more valuable the flowers are. Karl von Frisch, a German scientist who discovered this dance, won the Nobel Prize in 1973 for his work.

WORKER BEES

Most of the hive is made up of worker bees. Their job is to, well, do all the work!

When a worker bee emerges from her wax cell, she emerges weak and wet. But she gets right to work cleaning it. Then she immediately starts a sequence of activities. An adult worker bee's body keeps developing. As she grows, she takes on a series of jobs in a logical order. For the first three weeks of life, a worker starts as a nurse, feeding larvae. As she gets older, she starts performing other duties, such as cleaning out empty cells and cleaning dust off of other bees. She develops wax glands and chews wax into caps for pupa and honey cells. Next she serves as a guard bee, only allowing familiar-smelling bees back into the nest. If she senses danger, she releases an alarm pheromone to warn the hive. Guard bees may also sting creatures that threaten the hive. Finally, the worker starts flying out on collecting missions of about 3 miles (4.8 kilometers) in search of four substances: nectar, pollen, propolis, and water. Nectar, pollen, and water are needed for nutrition. Water also cools down the hive if it is too hot. Propolis is a sticky substance that bees develop from tree sap and other plants and use to seal cracks in hives.

In the height of the season, a worker may only live five or six weeks before she dies of exhaustion. Worker bees often die outside the nest. Until then, they are so busy that they hardly sleep!

CHAPTER THREE

BECOMING A BEEKEEPER

Tim Stewart has always been fascinated by bees. At ten, the New Jersey boy asked his father if he could start a beehive. A week later, his father saw a swarm of bees on a mailbox. He returned with Tim. "We got ourselves our first swarm," Tim told the *Press of Atlantic City*. After splitting the hives after the first winter, his bee business rapidly began to grow. At fourteen, he started Stewart's Apiaries. Today, he has more than two hundred hives!

Being a teen means that Tim has had few expenses. So he has been able to use his profits to build up his business. In addition to selling honey, he rents out his bees to pollinate local blueberries and cranberries. He also sells starter hives to other beekeepers.

Tim loves the learning process. "Right now I'd be better off making more honey...but I want to get into all of the different aspects," he told the newspaper.

A beekeeper proudly shows bees and honeycomb on a frame.

BEFORE STARTING BEEKEEPING

With adult help, young people can keep hives, though it's smart to follow Tim Stewart's example and start small. Find out if anyone in your family is allergic to bee stings. Contact a local beekeeping organization or group that teaches classes to beginning beekeepers. Staff or volunteers can explain what local laws affect beekeeping and explain what special equipment beekeepers need. There are beekeepers in organizations all over the United States and Canada that welcome questions and are almost as cooperative as bees themselves!

Then you'll need to collect the needed equipment. Some equipment useful for keeping bees includes:

- **Beekeeping outfit.** First, the beekeeper needs to dress up carefully in a bee-safe outfit. Buy a bee mask or veil with mesh netting to keep bees out of your face, and buy special protective clothing made for beekeepers. White is a good color. Some darker colors are annoying to bees, perhaps because they remind them of enemies in the wild. Tuck the pants into thick socks and shoes or boots. Wear thick gloves, and make sure they cover your wrists.

- **Langstroth frame.** Nineteenth-century beekeeper Lorenzo Langstroth cleverly determined just how much living space bees need: $3/8$ of an inch (.95 centimeters). He came up with the ingenious idea of keeping bees in cabinet-like spaces lined with vertical frames. These frames are spaced just far enough apart to allow bees to pass each other, do their multiple tasks in the dark, and stay warm.

Langstroth frames come in large, medium, and shallow sizes. Deep frames, or "deeps," are commonly used as bottom frames, where bees will spend most of their time, lay eggs, and tend to larvae. Sometimes beekeepers put up something called a "queen excluder" between the deeps and the frames that they place above them as the bottom frames get full. There is enough room for a worker bee to pass through but not the larger queen. That means these frames won't have any larvae—just pure honey.

The shallow frames are used when bees are producing a lot of honey by adding them to the top. To be safe, buy new frames from local, well-respected vendors. To avoid the possibility of infection, get new ones.

A bee smoker is an important tool because it helps calm bees down.

- **Smokers.** You will need smokers to calm the bees long enough to visit and, later, extract the honey from the hive. Cool, gentle smoke has two effects on bees: it makes them sleepy and it makes them hungry. Some flammable materials that beekeepers use include old rope, cow dung, and hay.
- **Bee tool.** This special knife will help you separate the frames so that you can lift them separately. Bees normally glue the frames shut with propolis, so the bee tool can help you cut through the sticky glue.

Getting the honey out of the hive is also important. For that you will need different equipment, which will be discussed later. This equipment, including a honey separator, is better

SWARMING

Sometimes, if a hive is getting too full and a new queen is born, a smaller group of bees divides and flies away from the nest, looking for a new home. This process is called swarming. Some lucky, skilled beekeepers can catch a swarm and fill new hives with one. However, the owner of the bees that swarmed loses those bees! Swarming can also put the bees in danger—sometimes they leave the hive and end up in bird boxes or vacuum cleaners. When inspecting bee frames, look for raised and lumpy swarm cells in the lower third of the frame. If there are eight or more, try adding more "supers" (smaller frames) on top of the bottom frames to give the hive room to grow.

When a hive feels overcrowded, bees can swarm. This can leave the bees extremely vulnerable until they find a new home.

borrowed or loaned from a local beekeepers' association than purchased because it is expensive and yet easy to share.

PLACING HIVES

Once beekeepers have equipment or know where to borrow it, the next step is picking the perfect spot to put the hives. It can mean the difference between success and failure for the colony. The following are some hints for placing hives.

Start on the sunny side! Make the opening face southeast. That way, the sun hits the hives earlier and the bees will start flying out sooner. A spot that has dappled sunlight gives a hive just the right amount of warmth and shade. Remember to keep the opening free of grass and weeds in the summer.

Hives should be placed where they won't get too much or too little wind. Trees or a hedge at the back of the hive can help protect against winter wind.

If the location is too damp, it can cause problems for the hive. When placing the hive, it should be level from side to side. But the front should be a little bit lower than the back so that water can drain out.

Finally, put the hives in a place where they are reachable when it's time to carry the frames for harvesting.

HANDLING WORRIED NEIGHBORS

One important aspect of being a good beekeeper is being respectful of the people who live nearby. Some may have bee allergies—or even just fear bees. So it is extra important to be a good neighbor, especially if you live close to other people. For example, bees are creatures of habit. They need water, and if you don't provide it for them, they may start visiting a neighbor's pool on a regular basis. That would definitely not be fun for your neighbors! So unless you have a natural source of water nearby, remember to put out a pan of fresh water for your bees regularly.

Having too many bees might annoy neighbors, too. For those who live in a densely packed area, one or two hives is probably enough. The direction of the opening of the hive can also make a big difference. If the opening points at a neighbor's front door, driveway, or doghouse, for instance, bees might get uncomfortably close to them. One way to prevent this is by putting up a fence or thick shrubbery that is at least 6 feet (1.8 meters) high. That way, the bees will not be tempted to fly in a straight line toward their next destination.

Another suggestion is—you guessed it—being sweet. Invite neighbors over to see the hive. Explain why bees are so fascinating. Tell them that bees can fly as far as 5 miles (8 km) away, so they don't have to worry about bees being around all the time. If the bees do hang around, they will pollinate neighbors' flower and vegetable gardens! Better yet, share the honey harvest. Give your neighbors jars of honey or bake them some honey-rich treats to thank them for their patience.

GETTING BEES AND STARTING A HIVE

The process of getting an order of bees and putting them into their new home is called hiving. Tim Stewart and his father were lucky—and skilled—enough to catch a swarm. But for most new beekeepers, the most convenient way to get new bees is to buy a whole colony at once through the mail.

One commonly sold unit is called a "nuc" (short for "nucleus colony"). A nuc is a smaller hive of three to five frames with bees. The nucleus, or center, of a beehive is the queen, and the nuc will have a queen so that the bees stay united as a colony. The frames can be added to a Langstroth hive easily. Use local suppliers with a good reputation.

Sixteen-year-old Orren Fox keeps four hives in a friend's yard in Massachusetts. "It's a cool sensation to have, like, twenty thousand bees flying around and landing on you. It's a sound like nothing I've ever heard." he told the *Boston Globe.*

Sadly, he lost three out of four hives last year. So he ordered some new ones: 9 pounds (4.1 kilograms), or about eighteen thousand bees. He and his mother experienced what many bee-keepers do—a very urgent phone call from the post office. His mother told the *Globe,* "The local post office calls very early in the morning and says, 'Your bees are here. Could you please come and *get them?'"* So, remember that if you order bees, be ready to pick them up right away!

Before getting bees, think about what species to purchase. Different species of honeybees have different personalities. Italian bees are known for their gentleness. Others are adapted to live in northern climates. Ask local beekeepers what kind of bees they recommend.

VISITING YOUR HIVE

Once the bees are settled, start checking on them weekly, starting mid-spring. Go on sunny, warm, calm days. Here are some tips:

- Shower first, but avoid smelly shampoo or soap, especially anything that smells like bananas. Leather smells bad to bees. So does wool.
- Wear a bee outfit, including a veil, and bring a smoker to calm them.
- Use a knife to pry propolis off the frames and separate them. Then lift up one frame at a time.
- Act calm. Swatting can make the bees feel threatened.

As spring develops, plant honeybee-loving plants near the hive to keep the bees close to home. During summer, check that the hives are healthy and have a queen.

Beekeepers have to make sure that their bees leave the frames before gathering honey.

PREPARING FOR WINTER

There are different times of the year when honey can be harvested, but August and September are often particularly good. After harvesting season, it's time to prepare the bees for winter. A colony in cold regions will need at least 60 pounds (27 kg) of capped honey to feed themselves, so don't take all the honey. If honey starts to run low, feed the bees sugar water in autumn, after all the blossoms are gone, so that they can convert it to honey for the winter.

In November, check for predators such as mice. Install an "entrance reducer" to keep them out. Putting a rock on top of the hive can keep it from tipping over from wind. Hives wrapped with black roofing tarpaper will stay warmer. From time to time, tilt the hives forward to allow water from rain and snow to run off.

Don't open the hives when the temperature is below 50 degrees Fahrenheit (10 degrees Celsius) during the day. Check the bees by tapping gently on the side—a buzzing sound means they're alive. Over the winter, make sure that snow doesn't block the entrance of the hive. Even though bees will mostly huddle in the hive, sometimes they need a bathroom break! Plus, if the entrance is clogged, they could suffocate. Check to make sure that they have access to water that isn't frozen, or place some water in a sunny location for them.

Eventually, the bees will form their winter cluster. Just know that inside the frame, the worker bees are using their body warmth to huddle around the queen and young. If all is well, no matter how icy it is outside, inside it will be toasty warm.

CHAPTER FOUR

TROUBLESHOOTING BEEKEEPING

Bees face a number of problems. In the 1940s, there were about five million managed honeybee colonies. Today, there are only about half that number, according to the USDA. Why are bees in trouble? Experts point to several possible problems.

COLONY COLLAPSE DISORDER

Starting in 2006, a number of beekeepers reported that a shocking number of their bees had died. The average loss of bees from 2006 to 2011 was about 33 percent each year, according to the USDA. In addition, their pattern of dying was unusual. In hives that seemed otherwise healthy and contained a queen, growing larvae, and honey, there were suddenly too few workers—not enough to keep the colony alive. Not only that, but it was also hard to find the bodies of any dead workers for scientists to analyze. They all seemed to have died far from the hive. Without enough workers, the colonies soon died.

This destroyed, abandoned hive shows the deadly effects of colony collapse disorder (CCD).

The U.S. Environmental Protection Agency (EPA) calls this combination of symptoms colony collapse disorder (CCD). Kevin Hackett of the USDA's bee and pollination program told Reuters, "This is the biggest general threat to our food supply."

One major culprit appears to be a new group of pesticides called neonicotinoids, also known as "neonics." They began to be popular just as bee colonies began to collapse. After studies, the EFSA, the top European food safety authority, called one of these pesticides, clothianidin, an unacceptable danger to bees.

European concerns are echoed by studies in the United States. An article in the journal *Science* showed these pesticides can damage bees' homing ability. Bee experts at Indiana's Purdue University said infected bees showed signs of pesticide poisoning. Scientists at Harvard actually recreated colony collapse disorder in several hives simply by giving them small doses of a neonic.

OUCH! WHEN BEES STING

Getting stung isn't fun. To handle a bee sting, the best technique is to get the stinger out as soon as possible, according to the USDA. Scrape the stinger with a fingernail or a credit card. Otherwise, it will continue to pump out toxins. Put ice or calamine lotion on the site, and take an antihistamine such as Benadryl. Drinking water helps. Still, a bee sting may hurt for several days.

Some people have to take a further step. If they are allergic to bees, or get stung by too many bees (more than fifteen bee stings, according to the USDA), they need to get medical attention. Some people are so allergic to bee stings that they may need to carry an EpiPen. This device provides a shot of a chemical called epinephrine to counteract their body's reaction to the bee sting. They may also need to go to the hospital immediately.

Heather Pilactic, co-director of the Pesticide Action Network, North America (PANNA), told the *Huffington Post*, "Neonicotinoids cover at least 142 million acres [57,465,361 hectares] of U.S. countryside, much of it corn...The most widely used of these neonicotinoids (imidacloprid, clothianidin, thiamethoxam) are known to be highly acutely toxic to bees, and have a variety of sublethal effects ranging from disorientation to memory, immunity, and reproductive impairment. These pesticides are clearly making bees sick."

So far, the EPA has said there is not enough proof to stop using neonics. So on March 21, 2013, a coalition of environmental groups and beekeepers filed a lawsuit against the EPA for registering these pesticides and allowing them to be used. According to Bloomberg.com, the coalition said neonics have been "repeatedly identified as highly toxic to honey bees, clear causes of major bee kills, and significant contributors to...colony collapse disorder." But bees face other dangers as well.

INFESTATION AND HABITAT FRAGMENTATION

Mice and other creatures such as bears can get into bees' nests, especially in the winter when they are hungry. Wasps can kill thousands of bees in a short amount of time. Make sure that there are openings large enough for bees to exit on warm days but not so large that other animals can get in.

Bees can also be hurt by creatures that are smaller than they are. According to an article on ScienceDaily .com, one big threat that honeybees face is infection from Varroa mites. These tiny creatures can spread a disease called deformed wing virus (DWV). Dr. Stephen Martin of the University of Sheffield in the United Kingdom said,

The bee on the left carries a mite on its thorax. Some mites are a serious threat to bees.

"Just two thousand mites can cause a colony containing thirty thousand bees to die. It's responsible for millions of bees being killed." Honeybees can also get an infection called foulbrood. When that happens, the only thing to do is burn the whole hive and bury it.

Some bees are trapped by habitat fragmentation. That means they are cut off from food and water supplies by buildings, highways, or other city obstacles. In the country, they can also be cut off from food and water supplies by monoculture—large pieces of land that are farmed with a single crop that can't provide for all their needs. Even large tracts of suburban grass can form a kind of monoculture that makes it hard for bees to survive. This has already led to the extinction of a number of wild bee species.

BEES GONE BAD

In 1957, a scientist in Brazil was studying a particular kind of African bee to see if it would produce a lot of honey in the South American tropics. But then, a few of these bees escaped, mated with other bees, and created a new kind of hybrid bee called the Africanized honeybee. Even though their venom is no more dangerous than that of other bees, they are far more aggressive. Whereas a normal bee might follow a threatening intruder for a short distance, swarms of enraged Africanized honeybees can chase their victims for a quarter of a mile (.4 km). These bees pose a threat to the rainforest by sucking up resources for the other bees. Now they have invaded parts of North America, including Florida, California, and as far north as Tennessee!

If those who live in an area with Africanized honeybees start getting chased by a swarm, experts have one piece of advice:

Africanized honeybees like this one are known for their aggressive behavior.

run, especially into the wind, until you reach shelter. Cover your face as much as possible with your shirt, don't swat, and don't jump into a swimming pool. "They'll wait for you to come up for air," said Bennie Watson, president of the Red River Valley Beekeepers Association, to the *Times Record News* of Wichita Falls, Texas. "You've got to get away from them as soon as possible. They just keep on attacking once they start."

CHAPTER FIVE

ALL ABOUT HONEY

oney is bees' most important food source. Bees gather nectar from flowers and pass it along to workers in the hive. These workers swallow it into their honey stomachs and spit it out repeatedly into empty hexagonal cells. This process adds special enzymes that help thicken the nectar and help transform it into honey. Even then it is not ready—it is still too wet. So other worker bees hover over the cells flapping their wings rapidly until enough of the liquid in the honey evaporates and it becomes the right consistency. Then it is thick enough to be sealed with a wax top.

PREPARING FOR THE HARVEST

Harvesting honey is a big job. It is one that beekeepers should prepare for carefully.

Be sure you have all the equipment that you need for the harvest. Some important honey harvesting items that you probably already own include a bucket of water and a dish towel

Two beekeepers smoke out a hive. Help can be useful at harvest time.

so you can wash off your hands frequently. You'll also want to have newspaper or a tarp to put on the floor. Extracting honey is messy work! Some other tools are more expensive, so you might want to rent or borrow them from a beekeeping club. They include:

- **An uncapping tool.** This helps cut the caps off the honey cells (in a pinch, a sharp bread knife works, too).
- **An uncapping tank.** This is a food-grade plastic container large enough to hold the bee frame over when cutting the caps off. It has a spigot for the honey that collects at the bottom along with the wax cuttings. It also has a crossbar on the top. Harvesters can rest

Beekeepers scrape wax lids off the honeycombs before adding them to a honey separator. The machine will spin, releasing honey until the frames are empty.

the frame on the crossbar while they're cutting.

• **A honey separator.** This machine spins honey out of a frame.

• **A large bucket with a cover.** This is helpful for storing honey for the first few days.

• **Jars and bottles for storing honey.** You can buy sterilized jars and labels from beekeeping suppliers, or use your own clean jars.

Once you have all the necessary supplies, you can begin to plan the harvesting process. To help the honey harvest flow smoothly, pick a good location. A garage, basement, or screened-in porch is a better place to do honey extracting than the kitchen. Make an exit near the top of a window so that stray bees can fly out.

Be cooperative! Honeybees work together to make honey. Harvesting is hard work. Get a friend or family member to help with the harvesting.

APITHERAPY

Ever drink tea with honey to soothe a sore throat? Many people believe that bee products, including honey, gathered pollen, royal jelly, propolis, and beeswax, have other health benefits, too. The use of bee products to treat illnesses or injuries is known as apitherapy. Some studies have shown that Australian Manuka honey has antibacterial qualities that can help with burns or acne. Honey has long been used as a folk medicine as well.

Researchers at the Washington University School of Medicine in St. Louis, Missouri, made nanoparticles (extremely tiny particles) of a toxic substance in bee venom called melittin. These particles are even smaller than HIV, the virus that causes AIDS. The scientists showed that the melittin nanoparticles can destroy HIV by poking holes in the virus's surface, while at the same time bouncing off normal cells. This discovery could lead to future AIDS-fighting drugs.

HARVESTING HONEY

When you are ready to harvest, say bye-bye to your bees! The last thing a beekeeper needs is thousands of mad bees clinging to the bee frame when she or he is harvesting. There are several ways to make bees flee their hives before you start getting the honey out. One is using a fume board. The board is soaked with a stinky chemical that bees hate. When it's placed inside the hive, bees fly out in large numbers. (They'll return when it's taken out.) Using a bee smoker also helps calm them down. Once the bees are gone, the frames can be removed from the hives.

DANGERS OF HONEY

Never feed honey to babies under the age of one. Honey can have tiny bacterial spores that could give babies a disease called infant botulism. This disease can affect their nervous systems. Even though older children and adults are also exposed to the spores, they are not usually affected by them.

Some honey is actually poisonous. Honey produced from the flowers of certain plants, including azaleas, mountain laurels, oleanders, and rhododendrons, may cause honey intoxication. Symptoms of this rare condition include dizziness, vomiting, and weakness.

Bring the honey frames to the uncapping tank. Place one of the frames over the large plastic container. Starting at the top, use the uncapping tool to slice the caps off the frame to release the honey from each cell. After uncapping, put the honey-filled frames into the honey separator until it is full. Start the machine. As it rotates, honey will fly out of the honeycomb and splash against the walls of the extractor. Then it will drip out into a bucket placed below.

After extracting the honey, cover it. Give it a few days to settle. Then bottle it. Store the honey at room temperature. If it's cloudy or has crystals, uncap the honey jar and put it in a microwave on low for a few minutes. Honey lasts for a long time if properly covered and stored. If it is uncovered, it can absorb oxygen and start to ferment.

WHAT TO DO WITH HONEY

Eat it! Sometimes the tastiest things to do with honey are the simplest because they let the special flavor of honey shine. Spoon it on plain yogurt and sprinkle walnuts on top. Add it to tea or warm milk. Spread it on English muffins or toast. Eat it Southern style, with fried chicken and waffles. Try it with apple slices. It can also be used in many baked goods instead of sugar. (Bakers should look up the appropriate substitutions because the amounts are slightly different than the amounts of sugar that one would use.) In addition, honey can be used for salad dressings and barbecue sauces. For honey recipes,

Honey is delicious on sliced bread, English muffins, pancakes, and many other foods.

visit the Web site of the National Honey Board at http://www .honey.com.

"Bee" beautiful! People can use honey to make their own skin and hair care products. For a natural way to dry pimples, smooth skin, and even out skin tone, try mixing the juice of half a lemon with two teaspoons of honey. Apply the mixture as a face mask and leave it on for twenty minutes. Rinse it off with cold water and dry it. Check the National Honey Board site for other simple "recipes" for smooth skin and shining hair.

ALL HONEYS ARE NOT THE SAME

Honey is classified in different ways. One way is by the kind of flowers from which the honeybees get their nectar. These monofloral (one flower) honeys include tupelo, buckwheat, clover, orange blossom, blueberry, and sage, among others. Another way honey is classified is by its color. According to the USDA's Pfund scale, "water white" honey is a zero, while "dark amber" honey is 114.

CHAPTER SIX

WHAT'S THE FUTURE FOR BEES?

Even bee lovers who don't want to start their own hives can take many actions to help these creatures have a healthy future. For those who want to take it even further, persuading other people to get together to fight for bees can strengthen their power. From school environmental clubs to 4-H to scouts, there are many organizations that bee lovers can join to advance the cause of these busy, fuzzy creatures.

There are also a number of things that people can do at home. Simple changes in the way that people live their daily lives can make a difference for bees.

PLANT A BEE-FRIENDLY GARDEN

Give bees a safe oasis by planting flowers for them. In the city, planting a window box, or even putting flowers in a pot, can help bees. People who live in the suburbs can either make a border or devote some garden space to bee-friendly flowers. Even easier,

Planting flowers and flowering trees, like this peach tree, gives bees a fighting chance to feed themselves and the hive.

leave a patch of your garden wild, or toss a package of wildflower seed mix in a bare corner.

Honeybees love dining on a wide variety of flowers. Just a few include peach, pear, and apple blossoms, goldenrod, wisterias, sunflowers, thistles, bee balm, cosmos, rosemary, and coneflowers. Planting early-flowering bulbs such as crocuses, daffodils, and snowdrops in the fall can give bees something to eat in early spring.

BE A SMART CONSUMER

Volunteer to go grocery shopping with your family and look at food labels. Try to buy fewer products with industrially produced corn products such as high-fructose corn syrup. They are more likely to contain neonics. Also, use honeys—especially local ones—to replace sugar whenever you can.

Eat organic, locally grown fruits and vegetables—the fewer pesticides, the better. Try recipes containing fresh, local produce and share them with family and friends. You can even try your own hand at starting a vegetable garden!

COUNT ON BEES

In 2008, biologist Gretchen LeBuhn of San Francisco State University started the Great Sunflower Project. She wanted to learn why bee populations were shrinking. She asked people around the country to plant a few sunflowers, in particular the Lemon Queen sunflower, available through her Web site. One hundred thousand volunteers have helped by counting the number of bees on a sunflower or other plant during two fifteen-minute observations per month. Participants report the data on LeBuhn's Web site, http://www.greatsunflower.org.

The Great Sunflower Project's Web site (http://www.greatsunflower.org) has a lot of interesting information and lets everyday people contribute to science.

Neonics are used in many home lawn and garden care products. They are even used in some flea treatments for cats and dogs. Volunteer to help with lawn care and try to use fewer pesticides. Landscaping services might use even more powerful forms of these pesticides, so ask what landscapers are using and let your family know if they're toxic.

GETTING TOGETHER

Honeybees work together to build and maintain a hive. Humans can harness the power of cooperation, too. Young people who love bees often have built-in networks that they can turn to for help. Whether it's school, 4-H or environmental clubs, or religious or other groups, bee lovers can get other people excited about helping bees. One idea is asking people to experiment with some of the previous suggestions at home. Other ideas include:

- **Create a buzz at school.** Ask to start a bee club at school, or make honeybee health a focus of an existing environmental club. Set up bulletin boards with bee facts and information on how to help bees. Create a PowerPoint presentation, Facebook page, or Web site to promote bees. Ask permission to start a bee garden on school property, or join the Great Sunflower Project.
- **Raise funds.** Get your group together to do fund-raisers for good causes such as the Foundation for the Preservation of Honey Bees (http://honeybeepreservation.org) or the Great Pollinator Project (http://greatpollinatorproject .org/Pollinator Project).

Standing up for bees helps people, too.

How can you raise money? Hold a bake sale, maybe with goods made with honey. Or have a honey taste-test party. Let people try different honeys on yogurt or vanilla ice cream. Cover up the label and let them vote on their favorites. Charge a small fee for participating.

Another idea is to invite a local beekeeper to speak at school or a club meeting. Charge a small admission fee, or ask for donations afterward. You can locate nearby beekeepers through *Bee Culture* magazine at http://www.beeculture.com/content/whoswho.

- **Be an activist.** Get out your keyboards and make your voices known. Get your club to write to the EPA to ban—or at least study—clothianidin. Contact information can be found at http://www.epa.gov/pesticides/regulating/contacts.htm. You can also write to your local representatives. Heather Pilactic of PANNA told the *Huffington Post*, "Decision makers still read the local papers, especially opinion pages. Get in the habit of writing letters to the editor."

IT'S NOT TOO LATE

As dire as the future can seem, there is hope. As environmentalist and author Bill McKibben wrote in his review of the book *Fruitless Fall*, "Past a certain point, we can't make nature conform to our industrial model. The collapse of beehives is a warning—and the cleverness of a few beekeepers in figuring out how to work with bees not as masters but as partners offers a clear-eyed kind of hope for many of our ecological dilemmas."

ANTENNAE The sensors on bees' heads that they use for smelling and touching.

APIARY An area where beehives are placed and cared for.

BEEBREAD Pollen mixed with honey or nectar and fed to larvae.

BEESWAX A substance that worker bees make with glands in their abdomens. They chew it into useful shapes, such as sheets of honeycomb, where they store eggs and honey.

BROOD The immature bees in a hive, including the eggs, larvae, and pupae.

CAP A wax covering on a cell of honeycomb. It covers honey or pupae.

COLONY A group of bees living together with one queen.

COMPOUND EYE An extra-large eye that has many sections. Bees have two compound eyes and three small ones.

DRONE A male bee, whose only job is to mate with the queen.

FORAGE To hunt or gather. Foraging bees search for pollen, nectar, propolis, and water.

GERM CELL A reproductive cell, which, when mature, can combine with another of the opposite sex to create offspring.

HIVE A place where social bees such as honeybees live and work together.

HONEY The main food produced and eaten by bees. Its main ingredient is nectar from flowers.

HONEYCOMB An area made of six-sided cells of beeswax where honey is stored and eggs are deposited.

INSECT An animal with an exoskeleton, three main body parts, and six legs.

LARVA A developing insect in its first stage after coming out of the egg.

MANDIBLE A mouthpart that worker bees use to chew wax and propolis.

NECTAR A sugary liquid made by flowers to attract insects like bees for pollination. The bees use nectar to produce honey.

PHEROMONE A chemical released by animals, especially insects, to encourage particular behaviors in other others of the same species.

POLLEN Small dustlike spores from a plant that are needed for reproduction.

POLLINATION The act of transferring pollen from one flower to another.

PROPOLIS A sticky plant fluid gathered by honeybees, used to seal cracks in the hive to keep out cold weather and diseases.

QUEEN BEE The hive's leader and the bee responsible for producing eggs.

ROYAL JELLY A milky white fluid produced by glands in the heads of worker bees. It is fed to larvae and the queen.

WAGGLE DANCE A dance that worker bees use to show other bees where nectar and flowers are located.

WORKER BEE A female member of a colony. These bees do almost all the work of the hive.

FOR MORE INFORMATION

American Bee Journal
51 S. 2nd Street
Hamilton, IL 62341
(217) 847-3324
Web site: http://www.americanbeejournal.com
American Bee Journal has been providing beekeeping information for at least 150 years. It has an online version,
plus a free Web site that offers tips, links, beekeeping
supplies for sale, fun facts, and more.

American Beekeeping Federation (ABF)
3525 Piedmont Road, Building 5, Suite 300
Atlanta, GA 30305
(404) 760-2875
Web site: http://www.abfnet.org
The American Beekeeping Federation is an organization for
professional and other beekeepers. It works with legislators
to help the beekeeping industry. Its Web site features bee
news, honey recipes, beekeeping advice, links for young
people, and other resources.

Canadian Association of Professional Apiculturalists (CAPA)
P.O. Box 373
Aylesford, NS BOP 1C0
Canada
Web site: http://www.capabees.org

CAPA is an association of professionals who work in the field of apiculture (beekeeping and bee management). Its work includes studying bees and pollination, collecting statistics, and sharing information about beekeeping in Canada.

Foundation for the Preservation of Honey Bees
P.O. Box 1445
Jesup, GA 31598-1445
(912) 427-4018
Web site: http://www.honeybeepreservation.org
The mission of this research and education foundation is preserving and protecting bees to ensure a quality food supply and environment. Its Web site provides reader-friendly information about bees and connects to resources on and off the Web.

Harry H. Laidlaw Jr. Honey Bee Research Facility
Bee Biology Road
University of California, Davis
One Shields Avenue
Davis, CA 95616
(530) 754-9390
Web site: http://beebiology.ucdavis.edu
This center provides important research focusing on basic bee biology and genetics. It addresses international concerns about bee health and meets the needs of California's multibillion-dollar agricultural industry. Its

Web site contains a wealth of information about bees and beekeeping, a kids' page, and a photo gallery.

National Honey Board (NHB)
11409 Business Park Circle, Suite 210
Firestone, CO 80504-9200
(303) 776-2337
Web site: http://www.nhb.org
This research and promotion board helps maintain and expand markets for honey and honey products. Its Web site provides honey research and data, instructions on how to store and take care of honey, and a variety of recipes for food and skin care with honey. It also has a local honey supplier locator.

WEB SITES

Due to the changing nature of Internet links, Rosen Publishing has developed an online list of Web sites related to the subject of this book. This site is updated regularly. Please use this link to access the list:

http://www.rosenlinks.com/UGFT/Beek

FOR FURTHER READING

Benjamin, Alison, and Brian McCallum. *Bees in the City: The Urban Beekeepers' Handbook.* London, England: Guardian Books, 2011.

Blackiston, Howland. *Beekeeping for Dummies.* 2nd ed. Hoboken, NJ: Wiley Publishing, 2009.

Brackney, Susan M. *Plan Bee: Everything You Ever Wanted to Know About the Hardest Working Creatures on the Planet.* New York, NY: Penguin, 2009.

Buchmann, Stephen L. *Honey Bees: Letters from the Hive.* New York, NY: Delacorte Press, 2010.

Cramp, David. *Beekeeping: A Beginner's Guide.* Oxford, England: Spring Hill, 2012.

Dixon, Luke. *Keeping Bees in Towns & Cities.* Portland, OR: Timber Press, 2012.

English, Ashley. *Keeping Bees with Ashley English: All You Need to Know to Tend Hives, Harvest Honey & More* (Homemade Living). New York, NY: Lark Crafts, 2011.

Flottum, Kim. *The Backyard Beekeeper: An Absolute Beginner's Guide to Keeping Bees in Your Yard and Garden.* Rev. & updated ed. Beverly, MA: Quarry Books, 2010.

Hopper, Ted. *Guide to Bees & Honey.* Brighton, England: Roundhouse Publishing Group, 2010.

Jacobsen, Rowan. *Fruitless Fall: The Collapse of the Honey Bee and the Coming Agricultural Crisis.* New York, NY: Bloomsbury, 2009.

Jones, Richard, and Sharon Sweeney-Lynch. *The Beekeeper's Bible: Bees, Honey, Recipes & Other Home Uses.* New York, NY: Stewart, Tabori & Chang, 2011.

Kidd, Sue Monk. *The Secret Life of Bees.* 10th anniversary ed. New York, NY: Penguin Books, 2011.

Kritsky, Gene. *The Quest for the Perfect Hive: A History of Innovation in Bee Culture.* New York, NY: Oxford University Press, 2010.

Marchese, Marina C. *Honeybee: Lessons from an Accidental Beekeeper.* New York, NY: Black Dog & Leventhal Publishers, 2009.

Markle, Sandra. *The Case of the Vanishing Honey Bees: A Scientific Mystery.* Minneapolis, MN: Millbrook Press, 2014.

Randall, Frank. *The Bee Book for Beginners.* Lake Erie, OH: Backyard Farm Books, 2012.

Sammataro, Diana, and Alphonse Avitabile. *The Beekeeper's Handbook.* 4th ed. Ithaca, NY: Comstock Publishing Associates, 2011.

Tautz, Jürgen. *The Buzz About Bees: Biology of a Superorganism.* New York, NY: Springer, 2009.

Turnbill, Bill. *Confessions of a Bad Beekeeper: What Not to Do When Keeping Bees* (with Apologies to My Own). New York, NY: The Experiment, 2011.

BIBLIOGRAPHY

Bedard, Paul. "Michelle Obama's Bees Ready for Spring."
USNews.com, March 23, 2010. Retrieved February 22,
2013 (http://www.usnews.com/news/blogs/washington
-whispers/2010/03/23/michelle-obamas-bees-ready-for-spring).

Brown, Joel. "A Natural Talent for Keeping Bees: Newburyport
Teen Gains Blog Followers with Tales of Bees, Chickens."
Boston Globe, July 5, 2012. Retrieved March 1, 2013
(http://www.boston.com/lifestyle/food/articles/2012/07/05/
newburyport_teen_expands_efforts_to_bee_keeping).

Bush, Michael. *The Practical Beekeeper: Beekeeping Naturally.*
Greenwood, NE: X-Star Publishing Company, 2011.

Elmore, Christina. "Teen Beekeeper Nominated for State Award."
Post and Courier, April 17, 2012. Retrieved March 5, 2013
(http://www.postandcourier.com/apps/pbcs.dll/article?AID=/
20120417/PC1606/120419387&slId=1&template=printart).

Fellow, Avery. "Beekeepers Sue EPA Over Pesticide Approvals."
Bloomberg.com, March 23, 2013. Retrieved April 1, 2013
(http://www.bloomberg.com/news/2013-03-22/beekeepers
-sue-epa-over-pesticide-approvals.html).

Frazier, Jim, Chris Mullin, Maryann Frazier, and Sara Ashcraft.
"Pesticides and Their Involvement in Colony Collapse
Disorder." eXtension.org, January 28, 2013. Retrieved March
5, 2013 (http://www.extension.org/pages/60318/pesticides
-and-their-involvement-in-colony-collapse-disorder).

Harbert, Jessica. "Henry's Honey: Teen Has a Passion for
Beekeeping." *Grow Northwest*, March 3, 2011. Retrieved

January 30, 2013 (http://www.grownorthwest.com/2011/
03/henry%E2%80%99s-honey-teen-has-a-passion-for
-beekeeping).

Horn, Tammy. *Beeconomy: What Women and Bees Can Teach
Us About Local Trade and the Global Market.* Lexington, KY:
University Press of Kentucky, 2012.

Lyon, William F., and James E. Tew. "Ohio State University
Extension Fact Sheet: Africanized Honey Bee, HYG-2124-97."
Ohioline. Retrieved March 10, 2013 (http://ohioline.osu.edu/
hyg-fact/2000/2124.html).

McDuffie, Jade. "Catching Up with Beekeeper Caroline Lowery."
Post and Courier, January 17, 2013. Retrieved April 1,
2013 (http://www.postandcourier.com/article/20130117/
PC1606/130119393).

National Honey Board. "The Story of Pollination." 2013.
Retrieved February 20, 2013 (http://www.honey.com/images/
uploads/general/broch-pollination.pdf).

Phys.org. "Global Prices of Pollination-Dependent Products
Such as Coffee Could Rise in the Long Term: Study." April
27, 2012. Retrieved February 10, 2013 (http://phys.org/
news/2012-04-global-prices-pollination-dependent-products
-coffee.html#jCp).

Post, Kevin. "Business Is Buzzing: Weymouth Township Teen
Produces, Sells Honey, Leases Bees for Pollination." *Press of
Atlantic City*, August 11, 2012. Retrieved March 5, 2013
(http://www.pressofatlanticcity.com/business/business-is

-buzzing-weymouth-township-teen-produces-sells-honey
-leases/article_76305f18-e348-11e1-8802
-0019bb2963f4.html).

PRWeb.com. "Where the Bees Are: Highland Hall Waldorf School
Supports Healthy Bees, Sustainable Farming, and Shares the
Green School Award from the Captain Planet Foundation." July
18, 2012. Retrieved February 20, 2013 (http://www
.prweb.com/releases/Wherethebeesare/highlandhall/
prweb9706039.htm).

Schiffman, Richard. "Mystery of the Disappearing Bees:
Solved!" Reuters, April 9, 2012. Retrieved March 5,
2013 (http://blogs reuters.com/great-debate/2012/04/09/
mystery-of-the-disappearing-bees-solved).

Seeley, Thomas D. *Honeybee Democracy.* Princeton, NJ:
Princeton University Press, 2010.

Skinner, John. "Are There Plants That Produce Nectar That
Is Poisonous to Either Honey Bees or Humans?" eXten-
sion.org, November 10, 2009. Retrieved February 10,
2013 (http://www.extension.org/pages/44129/are-there
-plants-that-produce-nectar-that-is-poisonous-to-either
-honey-bees-or-humans).

Spiegelman, Annie. "Bee Deviled: Scientists No Longer Bumbling
Over Cause of Colony Collapse Disorder." *Huffington Post*,
September 19, 2012. Retrieved June 1, 2013 (http://www
.huffingtonpost.com/annie-spiegelman/bee-deviledscientists
_b_1884294.html).

Strait, Julia Evangelou. "Nanoparticles Loaded with Bee Venom Kill HIV." Washington University in St. Louis, March 7, 2013. Retrieved March 12, 2013 (http://news.wustl.edu/news/Pages/25061.aspx).

UC Davis Department of Entomology and Nematology. "Honey Bees Are More Effective at Pollinating Almonds When Other Species of Bees Are Present." January 10, 2013. Retrieved March 1, 2013 (http://entomology.ucdavis.edu/News/Honey_Bees_Are_More_Effective_at_Pollinating_Almonds_When_Other_Species_of_Bees_Are_Present).

University of Sheffield. "Highly Contagious Honey Bee Virus Transmitted by Mites." ScienceDaily.com, June 7, 2012. Retrieved March 5, 2013 (http://www.sciencedaily.com/releases/2012/06/120607142357.htm).

U.S. Department of Agriculture, Agricultural Research Service. "Honey Bee Research: Africanized Honey Bees." November 10, 2011. Retrieved March 20, 2013 (http://www.ars.usda.gov/Research/docs.htm?docid=11059).

U.S. Department of Agriculture, Agricultural Research Service. "Honey Bee Research: Bee Stings/Safety." April 26, 2012. Retrieved March 20, 2013 (http://www.ars.usda.gov/Research/docs.htm?docid=11075).

U.S. Department of Agriculture, Agricultural Research Service. "Honey Bees and Colony Collapse Disorder." May 7, 2013. Retrieved June 1, 2013 (http://www.ars.usda.gov/News/docs.htm?docid=15572#losses).

Warner, Amanda. "Beekeepers Warn of Summer Threat."
    Times Record News, April 21, 2009. Retrieved March 30,
    2013 (http://www.timesrecordnews.com/news/2009/apr/21/
    beekeepers-warn-of-summer-threat).
Weichselbaum, Simone. "Brooklyn Bees Buzzing Hard for
    the Honey-Heavy Jewish New Year." *New York Daily
    News*, September 10, 2012. Retrieved February 20,
    2013 (http://www.nydailynews.com/new-york/brooklyn/
    brooklyn-bees-buzzing-hard-honey-heavy-jewish-new-year
    -article-1.1156164).

INDEX

A

Africanized honeybees, 34–35
apitherapy, 39

B

beebread, 17
Bee Culture magazine, 48
beekeepers, commercial, 9–11
beekeeping
 equipment/clothing, 21–25
 getting bees and starting a hive,
  26–27
 handling worried neighbors, 25–26
 legality of, 10
 placing hives, 25
 preparing for winter, 29
 visiting your hive, 27–28
bee stings/allergies, 15, 21, 25, 32

C

clothianidin, 31, 32, 48
colony collapse disorder (CCD),
  30–31, 33
complete metamorphosis, 17

D

deformed wing virus (DWV), 33
drones, 16, 18

E

EpiPen, 32
exoskeleton, 14

F

foulbrood, 34
Foundation for the Preservation of
  Honey Bees, 4, 6, 46
Fox, Orren, 27
Frisch, Karl von, 6, 18
fume boards, 39

G

Great Pollinator Project, 46
Great Sunflower Project, 45, 46

H

habitat fragmentation, 34
Hackett, Kevin, 31
hives, overview of, 15–16
hiving, 26
honey
 classification of, 42
 dangers of, 40
 havesting honey, 29, 39–40
 preparing for the harvest/equipment,
  36–38
 what to do with honey, 41–42

honeybees
 anatomy of, 13–15
 eyes/vision, 14
 history of, 4–5
 life cycle of, 16–17
 social behavior of, 13
 threats to, 30–34
honeybees, types of,
drones, 16, 18
queen bee, 10, 15, 16, 17–18, 22,
  24, 27, 28
worker bees, 8, 16, 17, 18, 19, 22
honey intoxication, 40
honey separator, 23, 38, 40

I

infant botulism, 40

L

Langstroth, Lorenzo, 22
Langstroth frames, 22, 27
Lautenbach, Sven, 9
LeBuhn, Gretchen, 45
Lowery, Caroline, 12

M

Martin, Stephen, 33–34
McKibben, Bill, 48
melittin, 39
Miller, Henry, 4, 6

N

nectar, 7, 15, 18, 19, 36
neonicotinoids/neonics, 31–33, 44, 46
nuc/nucleus colony, 27

O

Obama, Michelle, 12
ocelli, 14
ommatidia, 14

P

pesticides/insecticides, 8, 31–33,
  44, 46
pheromones, 17–18, 19
Pilactic, Heather, 32, 48
pollen, 7, 14, 15, 17, 19, 39
pollination, 6, 7, 8–9, 12
propolis, 19, 23, 28, 39

Q

queen bee, 10, 15, 16, 17–18, 22,
  24, 27, 28
queen excluder, 22

R

Rosh Hashanah, 10
royal jelly, 17, 39

S

smokers, 23, 28, 39
spermatheca, 18
Stewart, Tim, 20, 21, 26
swarming, 24

U

uncapping tools and tanks, 37–38, 40

V

Varroa mites, 33–34

W

wasps, 13, 33
Watson, Bennie, 35
worker bees, 8, 16, 17, 18, 19, 22

ABOUT THE AUTHOR

Alexandra Hanson-Harding has always found the creepy, tiny world of insects fascinating. She loves watching bees buzzing in the amazing garden her husband plants in the backyard each year, which yields green beans, tomatoes, bok choy, and many other wonderful, well-pollinated plants. Ms. Hanson-Harding has written hundreds of articles and many books for children and adults on topics ranging from social studies to life skills to science. She lives in New Jersey with her husband, two sons, and cat.

PHOTO CREDITS

Cover, back cover © iStockphoto.com/HPuschmann; cover, back cover Chris Clinton/Getty Images; p. 5 © Denise Miller; p. 8 Daniel Prudek/Shutterstock.com; pp. 9, 33, 35, 47 © AP Images; p. 10 Dmitrydesign/Shutterstock.com; p. 11 Kathryn Scott Osler/Denver Post/Getty Images; p. 14 abxyz/Shutterstock.com; p. 16 Donna Hayden/Shutterstock.com; p. 17 Steve Hopkin/Taxi/Getty Images; p. 21 Anthony Lee/OJO Images/Getty Images; p. 23 Jaime Kowal/FoodPix/Getty Images; p. 24 zhang bo/E+/Getty Images; p. 28 Monty Rakusen/Cultura/Getty Images; p. 31 Penn State Univ/Science Source; p. 37 Cavan Images/Photonica/Getty Images; p. 38 Thomas Frey/picture-alliance/dpa/AP Images; p. 41 William Berry/Shutterstock.com; p. 44 Natasa Adzic/Shutterstock.com; p. 45 © The Great Sunflower Project; cover and interior pages (cityscape silhouette) © iStockphoto.com/blackred; cover and interior pages (dirt) © iStockphoto.com/wragg; back cover and interior pages (beehive silhouette) © iStockphoto.com/dedMazay; interior pages (silhouette texture) © iStockphoto.com/mon5ter.

Designer: Nicole Russo; Editor: Andrea Sclarow Paskoff;
Photo Researcher: Marty Levick